SCHIRMER'S LIBRARY
OF MUSICAL CLASSICS

FRANZ LISZT

Twelve Songs
For Voice and Piano

With a Critical Note by
RICHARD ALDRICH

The English Translations by
DR. THEODORE BAKER

FOR LOW VOICE
Library Volume 1613

FOR HIGH VOICE
Library Volume 1614

G. SCHIRMER, Inc.

DISTRIBUTED BY
HAL•LEONARD®
CORPORATION
7777 W. BLUEMOUND RD. P.O. BOX 13819 MILWAUKEE, WI 53213

FRANZ LISZT
A CRITICAL NOTE BY
RICHARD ALDRICH

Franz Liszt's marvellous career brought him into intimate relations with all sides of his art. It was a career of fascinating brilliancy, marked by strongly contrasted episodes; of invincible success in most things that the world counts as success; of changing and advancing ideals; of strivings that lifted him ever higher and higher toward nobler conceptions of the functions of an artist. We find him first a virtuoso of perhaps the highest genius that the world has ever seen; a composer of bravura pianoforte pieces that only his technical powers could approach. We see then a deeper influence gaining control over his activities, turning him to the most serious forms of composition, to a philosophic consideration of problems underlying the æsthetics of music, and to an effort to lead his art into new paths, to establish new forms and set up new ideals. There is something profoundly impressive in the spectacle of this man, at the climax of the most triumphant career that a musician ever had, suddenly renouncing all the worldly success it brought him, and withdrawing from its allurements to devote himself to preaching a new evangel of art. He established himself as conductor of the opera and orchestra at the Court theatre of Weimar, with the distinct purpose of becoming the advocate of the new school of music, of forwarding with the prestige of his great name and the resources of his position the claims of an unpopular and misunderstood group of composers, whose works had otherwise little chance of a hearing; and at the same time he enlisted with enthusiasm under this same banner as a composer, fired with the same enthusiasms and animated by the same views of the artistic ideal. The close of Liszt's career as a virtuoso and the beginning of his activity at Weimar occurred at the end of the year 1841; and from about the same period of his life is to be dated his concern with the higher functions of creative art, and the beginning of a long series of compositions that have had a marked influence on the development of music. Among the great mass of the works of these maturer years his songs hold an important place.

It was distinctively a German ideal that he followed in this later development of his genius. This fact is clearly visible in his songs. They number more than sixty; with a very few exceptions they were conceived and composed on German soil, are settings of German poems, and, while essentially individual in their embodiment of Liszt's own genius, show plainly the influence of the German masters of song. In the late summer of 1841—he was then thirty years old—he took up his abode on the island of Nonnenwerth, in the Rhine. It is significant of the influence always exerted upon him by his environment that his first composition during his communing with the sacred river of Germany should be a setting of Heine's poem, " Die Lorelei." He had hitherto published but one song, a setting of Italian verse to music, unmistakably Italian in its quality, " Angiolin dal biondo crin "—another hint of the receptivity of his nature—that he had composed during a sojourn at Rome. The " Lorelei " was followed by a series of songs to words by Goethe, Schiller, Heine, Rückert, Geibel, Bodenstedt, Lenau, Hoffmann von Fallersleben, and other German poets. In 1842 he published a set of French songs chiefly to poems by Victor Hugo, which, according to his biographer, Fraulein Ramann, he had already conceived in Paris, and which bear in themselves traces of their French origin; but with this exception, the sixty odd songs that followed, written on his Rhine island and during his career at Weimar, are an endeavor to give voice to the German spirit and to interpret German ideals.

These songs have not escaped the fate of Liszt's other compositions in becoming the subject of great debate and controversy. They belonged to the " path-breaking " productions of the young German composers, who were trying to revolutionize the art of music and enlarge its boundaries; and as such they came in for the general condemnation with which the conservatives fought the new movement. But since the smoke and noise of that conflict have in large measure passed away, Liszt's claims to recognition as a creative genius, as a composer, have been resisted even by ardent supporters of the cause he espoused. Only a small proportion of his works has found wide acceptance from the musical public, and, with comparatively few exceptions, the songs are among the less known. Some of them, such as " Die Lorelei," " Du bist wie eine Blume," and " Es muss ein Wunderbares sein," have gained a large measure of popularity. But it may be truly said of all of them that they are as entirely representative of the composer's aims, methods, and inspiration as any of his compositions, both in their melodic quality and in their form and structure.

Most of these songs embody in the highest degree the dramatic idea—the abandonment of the purely strophic form of continuous melody in favor of a method of procedure that shall more accurately expound the changing sentiment of the text. Verse by verse, almost word by word, we find the music in them subordinated to the poem through changes of melodic motive, or the interruption of the melodic sequence with sudden breaks into declamatory passages; frequent differentiations of the tempo, shiftings of rhythm and of tonality, sometimes by adventurous modulations, sometimes by still bolder plunges into new keys without modulation; and everywhere the elaboration of the piano-forte accompaniment as an essential factor in the musical development. There are constant reminders of Liszt's anxiety that exactly the right shade of meaning shall be given by the singer. Besides the fullest use of ordinary marks of expression, he gives directions in various languages as to the minutest details of performance. The half-spoken style is a favorite of Liszt's, as may be gathered from the frequent appearance on his pages of such hints as " decla-mirt," " gesprochen," and " fast gesprochen," " parlando," " parlé;" he is frequently explaining just the dramatic nuance, accent, and vocal coloring he desires with such prescriptions as " mit halber Stimme," " bestimmt," " ernst," " düster," " schwungvoll," " geheimnissvoll," " phlegmatisch," " hinträumend," " schwankend," " sehr accentuirt," " vibrato," " pronunziato assai," and so on. And, indeed, it is quite essential for the realization of the spirit in which Liszt conceived his songs that the singer should be guided by these directions to a perfectly free and dramatically flexible style of performance.

Here we have reached, as the distinguished English critic, Dr. Hueffer, has said, the consistent carrying-out of the poetic principle in lyric music to its final consequences.

Liszt has freed himself entirely from any reverential feeling for the abstract sacredness of the musical form; "he is a poet and nothing but a poet." He has endeavored to embody in the smaller frame of the song the principle that Wagner laid down for the lyric drama; that the means of expression, the music, should not be made the end; that the object of the expression, the drama—represented now by the poem— should not be made the means. The music must lend itself unreservedly and continuously to intensifying the emotional content of the text; the text must not be a mere peg upon which to hang a tune. Others before Liszt had found that a strict adherence to the strophic form in the art-song was often impossible, and the " durchcomponirtes Lied "— the song in which the whole musical tissue is more or less modified to suit the changing sentiment of the verse—had justified itself to Schubert and even to Beethoven. None, however, had ever carried the principle to so complete a working-out as Liszt. That there is danger to the essentials of artistic unity and consistent development of the musical element in the extent to which he carried it, has been admitted by even ardent admirers of Liszt's methods and ideals. There is danger that not only the musical beauty, but the rhythmic organism of the poem may be injured, as Dr. Hueffer has pointed out. Liszt himself found numerous occasions when such a course did not suggest itself to him, as is seen in his purely lyric settings, such as those of " Du bist wie eine Blume " and " Es muss ein Wunderbares sein." Whether or not he has sometimes passed beyond the boundaries that circumscribe the true limits of song, is still a question unsettled. We cannot do better in stating the position of his followers than to quote still further the opinion of the eminent English critic just referred to, who, in an analysis of the song, "Am Rhein," justifies Liszt in these words:

" The perfect blending of the two arts strikes the hearer with a feeling of beauty and harmony of a higher order, because it arises from the mutual surrender of two divergent elements in one common effort. In works like this Liszt has brought the efficiency of music for poetical purposes to a pitch formerly unknown in lyrical compositions."

RICHARD ALDRICH.

CONTENTS

Mignon's Lied
Song of Mignon

Poem by Goethe
English Tranlation by
Dr. Theo. Baker

Franz Liszt
Original key F♯ major

Kennst du das Land, wo die Ci-tro-nen blüh'n, im
Know'st thou the Land where-in the ci-trons bloom? The

dun-keln Laub die Gold-o-ran-gen glüh'n,   ein sanfter Wind vom
gold-en or-ange glows in_ leaf-y gloom;   From a-zure skies the

blau-en Him-mel weht, die Myr - the still und hoch der Lor - beer steht?
breez-es gen-tly lave The myr - tle hush'd, and high the_ lau - rels wave.

Printed in the U.S.A.

rall.

lieb - ter, mit dir, o mein Ge-lieb-ter, zieh'n.
lov - ed, with thee, with thee I'd fain re - pair!

Kennst du das Haus? Auf Säu - len ruht sein Dach; es glänzt der
Know'st thou the House? be - hind its pil - lar'd walls How light the

Saal, es schimmert das Ge - mach, und Mar-mor-bil-der
rooms, re-splendent shine the halls, And mar-ble stat-ues

steh'n und seh'n dich an; was hat man dir, du ar - mes Kind, ge-
stand and gaze on thee: Poor child, what sor-rows blight thy des-ti-

hin   mit   dir,   o mein ___ Be -
there,   I'd   fain,   my own ___ be -

schüt - zer,   mit   dir,   o mein Beschützer, zieh'n.
lov - ed,   with   thee, with thee I'd fain re-pair!

a tempo Più mosso.

Kennst   du _____   den Berg   und
Know'st   thou _____   the Mount,   whose

sei - nen Wol - ken-steg?   Das   Maul - thier sucht   im
path in clouds up-winds?   The   mule   on mist - y

Es war ein König in Thule.
There was a king in Thule.

Poem by Goethe.

Original key.

Es war ein Kö-nig in Thu-le, gar treu bis an sein
There was a king in Thu-le, E'er faith-ful to the

Grab, _____ dem ster - bend sei - ne Buh-le ei-nen gold'nen Becher
grave, _____ Whose la - dy-love,when dy-ing, Him a gold-en beak-er

gab, ei-nen gold'nen Be-cher gab. Es ging ihm Nichts dar-
gave, him a gold-en beak-er gave. At ev-'ry feast he____

poco rall.

ü - ber, er leert' ihn je - den Schmaus, _____ die Au-gen gin - gen ihm
drain'd it, Naught else did he so prize, _____ And ev-'ry time that he

poco rall.

Ped.

a tempo

ü - ber, so oft er trank dar - aus, so oft er trank dar -
quaff'd it The tears o'er-ran his eyes, the tears o'er-ran his

a tempo

aus. Und als er kam zu
eyes. And when his end was

p

ster - ben, zählt' er sei - ne Städt' im Reich,
near - ing, His domains he count - ed all,

dim.

gönnt' al - les sei - nen Er - ben, den Be - cher nicht zu -
Will'd them a - way full light - ly, But not the cup, with -

gleich,
al,
gönnt' al - les sei-nen Er - ben,den Be-cher nicht zu -
Will'd them a-way full light - ly, But not the cup, with-

cresc.

gleich.
al.
Er sass beim Königs-mah-le,
He held a roy-al banquet,
die Rit - ter um ihn
With knights on either

her
side,
auf hohem Vä-ter - saa-le,
In his fore-fa-thers' castle,
dort auf dem Schloss am
Yon by the o-cean-

Allegro agitato.

Meer.
tide.

Dort   stand   der al - te__
Up - rose   the a - ged__

Ze - cher,   trank   letz - te Le - bens - gluth,   und   warf   den heil' - gen
rev - 'ler,   Life's   part - ing glow   to__   drain;   Then   hurl'd   the hal - low'd

Be - cher   hin - un - ter   in   die Fluth,   hin - un - ter   in   die
beak - er   Far out - ward   in   the main,   far out - ward   in   the

14

riten.

Die Au - gen thä - ten ihm sin - - - ken.
His eyes grew dim - mer and dim - - - mer.

p riten.

dim.

Trank nie ei - nen Trop - fen mehr,
Drank he nev - er - more, I trow,

p

riten.

p

trank nie ei - nen Trop - fen mehr.
drank he nev - er - more, I trow.

p

p a tempo

rit.

„Es muss ein Wunderbares sein„

It must be wonderful, withal

Poem by Redwitz.

Original key.

Schwebend.
Con elevazione.

Es muss ein Wun - der - ba - res
It must be won - der - ful, with -

sein ums Lie - ben zwei - er See - len, sich schlie - ssen
al, When two, with hearts con - fid - ing, Are each to

ganz ein - an - der ein, sich nie ein Wort ver - heh - len,
oth - er all in all, Nor e'en a thought are hid - ing.

dolce

und Freud und Leid___ und Glück und Noth___ so mit ein-
In joy or pain,___ in weal or woe___ With each the

poco rit.

an - der tra - gen, so mit ein - an - der tra - gen;
oth - er bear - ing, with each the oth - er bear - ing,

poco rit. e cresc.

dolce   smorz.

vom er - sten Kuss bis in den Tod___ sich nur von Lie - be
From first fond kiss till death lay low,___ In love a - lone still

pp rit.

langsamer
più lento

sa - gen, sich nur von Lie - be sa - gen.
shar - ing, in love a - lone still shar - ing.

pp

Freudvoll und leidvoll

Joyful and Woeful

Poem by Goethe.

Original key.

39660

Die Schlüsselblumen

Aus „Mutter Gottes Sträusslein
zum Maimonate."

Poem by Joseph Müller.

The Primroses

From "The Virgin Mary's Nosegay
for the Month of May."

Original key.

mit dem Veilchen um die Wet - te würzen sie die lin - de Luft.
Vy - ing with the ear - ly vi - o - let They perfume the balm - y air.

Sie, des Len - zes er - ste Kin - der
They, the spring - tide's ear - liest chil - dren,

sind gar frü - he schon erwacht, stie - gen aus des Gra - bes Dun - kel,
Do be - times their eyes un - close, From the gloom - y earth a - ris - ing

eh' der O - ster - mor - gen tagt, sie erschlos - sen froh die Er - de
Ere the East - er sun a - rose. At the first warm sigh of spring - time

bei des Len-zes er-stem Weh'n
Glad their fet-ters off they shake,

und ver-kün-den,
And they tell, the

dass sie na-he, al-ler Blü-then Auf-ersteh'n,
time is near-ing When the flow'rs shall all a-wake,

und ver-kün-den, dass sie na-he,
And they tell, the time is near-ing

al-ler Blü-then Auf-er-steh'n.
When the flow'rs shall all a-wake.

Langsamer
Meno mosso

Die-se Blümchen lass ein Zei-chen, Him-melskö-ni-gin, dir sein,
May these flow'rets be a to-ken, Queen of Heav'n, to thee a-bove,

Andante.

In Liebeslust.

In Love's Delight.

Poem by
Hoffmann von Fallersleben.

Schnell - sehr bewegt und glühend.
Allegro, molto agitato ed ardente.

Original key A♭ major.

Die Loreley
Loreley

Poem by Heine
English translation by
Dr. Theo.Baker

Franz Liszt
Original key G major

Nicht schleppend
Moderato. (Non strascinando)

Ich weiss nicht, was soll's be-deu-ten, dass ich so trau - rig, so trau - rig
I know not what-e'er pre-sa-ges, That fills my heart, my heart with

bin.   Ein Märchen   aus
woe;   A sto-ry   of

al - ten Zei-ten, das kommt mir nicht aus dem Sinn, das kommt mir nicht___
by - gone a - ges Now haunts me, nor will it go, now haunts me, nor___

poco rit.

o - ben wunder-bar, ihr gold'- nes Ge-schmeide blit- zet, sie
maid - en wondrous fair, In gold - en ar - ray she shin - eth, And

poco rall. *sempre dolce*

kämmt — ihr gold'- nes Haar; sie kämmt es mit gold'nem Kam - me und
combs — her gold - en hair; Of gold is the comb she wield - eth, And

poco rall. *sempre dolcissimo*

singt — ein Lied da - bei, das hat ei - ne wun-der-sa - me,
e'er — she sings a lay O'er-pow'r - ing the heart that yield - eth

cresc.

cresc. molto

ge - walt' - ge Mel-o - dei, ge - walt' - ge Mel-o -
To marv - 'lous mel-o - dy, to marv - 'lous mel-o -

string. *tre corde*

"Du bist wie eine Blume"

"Ah, sweet as any flower"

Poem by Heine.

Original key A major.

Langsam, innigst.
Adagio con molto affetto.

Voice.

Piano.

Du__ bist wie ei - ne
Ah,__ sweet as__ an - y

Blu - me, so hold__ und schön und rein. Ich__
flow - er, And fair__ and pure thou art. I__

schau' dich__ an, und Weh - muth schleicht mir__ in's Herz hin - ein.
gaze on__ thee, and mourn - ful Fore - bod - ing fills__ my heart.

Oh! Quand je dors

O, while I sleep

Poem by Victor Hugo.

Original key E major.

ra,_____ ray - on - ne - ra!_____
shine,_____ my dream, will shine!_____

Puis, sur ma lè - vre, où vol-tige u - ne flam - me, É-clair d'a -
Then press thy lips up - on mine, where is burn - ing A flame of

mour_____ que Dieu même _____ é - pu - ra,
love _____ that bears no _____ base al - loy,

Pose____ un bai - ser, et d'an - ge de-viens
Thou____ an - gel fair, to wo - man's im - age

S'il est un charmant gazon

If there be a charming lawn

Poem by Victor Hugo.

Original key A♭ major.

S'il est un rê - ve d'a - mour
If there be a lov - er's dream,

Par - fu - mé de
Fraught with balm of

ro - se,
ros - es,

Où l'on trou - ve cha - que jour
Where from day to day supreme

Quelque dou - ce cho - se;
New de - light un - clos - es,

Un rê - ve que Dieu bé - nit,
A dream that our Lord has blest,

Où l'â - me à l'â - me s'u - nit,
Where heart within heart find - eth rest,

Oh! j'en veux
Oh, there I

„Kling' leise, mein Lied"

Breathe lightly, my lay

Poem by Nordmann.

Original key B major.

Die drei Zigeuner
The Three Gypsies

Poem by Lenau.

English version by
Philip J. Mosenthal.

Original key.

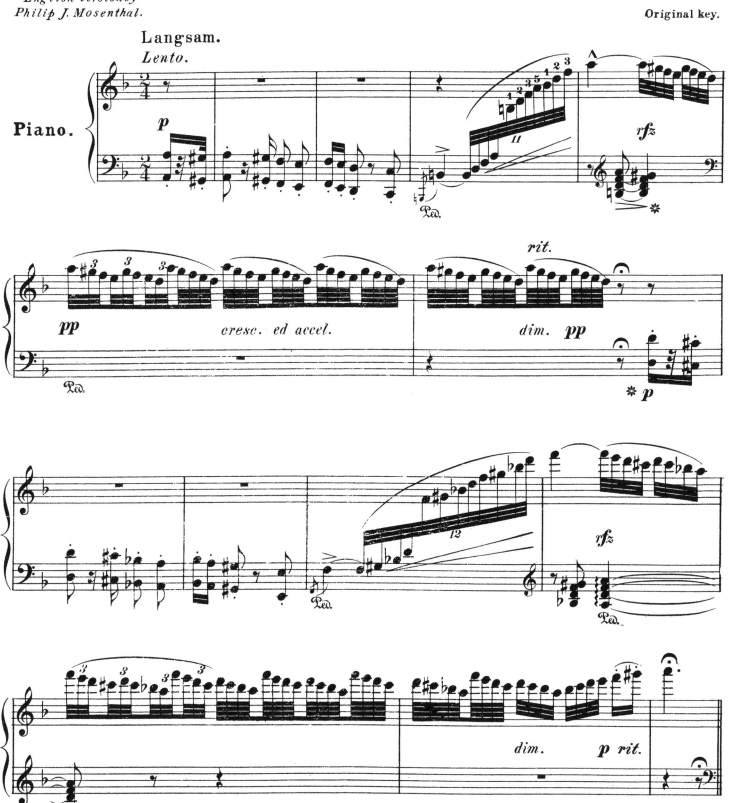

gesprochen
parlando

Drei Zi - geu - ner fand ich ein - mal lie - gen an ei - ner Wei - de, als mein
Gypsies three were ly - ing one day, By_ a wil - low re - pos - ing, While I

p un poco marc.

cresc.

Fuhr - werk mit mü - der Qual_ schlich durch san - di - ger Hai -
trudg'd on my wea - ry way,_ Tired, for day - light was clos -

cresc.

de.
ing.

rfz

accel.

(Trillo)
(lungo.)

Ped. Ped. Ped.

Allegro vivace quasi presto.

Hielt der Ei - ne für sich al-lein in den Hän - den die
One, he played for him-self a -lone, Fiddling free - ly and

Fie - dèl, spielt'____ um - glüht vom A - bend -
lithe - ly, Fad - ing____ light a - round him

schein____ sich____ ein lu - sti - ges Lie - del.
shone,____ Sing - ing his dit - ty so blithe - ly.

57